# Survival Activities For Children

By:
Edna Stowell

These are activities for people that want to help their children learn different survival skills. This is a reference book on some basic survival skills for children and their parents to learn together.

Survival/ Prepping Series

SHTF: Home schooling workbook
K-2

What is a bug out bag

Top 10 things to start prepping

All books are available on
Amazon.com and
createspace.com

Prepare for the worst by hope for the best.

# Activity 1

This activity has several different ways it can  be done depending on how many children you are working with at the time of  activity. So I will break this activity into different parts and you can use the parts that best work for your child/children.

Step 1:

The first step in this activity is very easy. Take your child/children to a place that they would normal spend time. Have you child/children listen to the sounds around them. These sound will change over time so have them do this everyday for a week. After the your child/children have listened for 10 minutes have them tell you what they heard.(You can also give them a journal to write down what they hear and if the sounds change on different days.) Ask your child/children if the sound was same or different then the other days they have listened. If the child/children said that something that was different have them tell you why this change may have happened.

Step 2:

Take a walk with your child/children and have them talk about the different sounds they hear as they walk long. (If they have a journal to take notes in this may help them remember things day to day to note any changes they hear.)

After doing step one and two for a week or more them move onto the next step. But only when your child/children are ready to move on to the next step make sure your child/children feel ready to move onto the next step.

Step 3:
(for a group)

Have your children form a circle. Then have one child stand in the middle of the circle. You can blindfold the child in the center of the circle or just have them close their eyes. Then have one child at a time walk towards to child in the center. Have them try to touch the child in the center without that child hearing them coming. If the child in the center turns towards the sound of the  child that is walking towards them that child most freeze and then return to the outer circle. Then the next child will try to get near the child in the center. This keeps going until all the children in the outer circle have had a chance to try to get the child in the center or a child touches the child in the center. Go thru this with every child in the circle. This will let you know what children need more time listening to the sounds around them.

Step 4:
(for a group)

Have the children in the

group form two lines a crossed from each other. Then one at a time have the a child from the group walk between the two lines blindfolded. Have the children in the line make different noises as the child walk thru the line. At the end of the two lines have the child that walked between the two lines tell you the sounds they heard when they were walking. Continue doing this until all the children have walked in between the lines.

*This activities will help your child/children learn to listen to their surroundings. This could help them if someone tries to come up behind them .*

## Activity 2

This is a very basic activity so much that the basics are sometimes taught in schools. Map  and compass reading can be a very helpful in a survival event. It may also be helpful to teach your child/children how to draw a basic map.

Step 1:

Map reading is a skill that can be helpful in both survival and non-survival life. Make sure that your child/children can read the map key and scale.

Step 2:

Have your child/children draw a basic map of their room. Once they show that they understand how to read and draw a map. Have them hide something outside on your yard and draw you a map to help you find the object.

Step 3:

Show your child/children a compass and how the needle always points north.

Step 4:

Take your child/children for a walk in the woods. Give them a compass to use during the walk, As you walk with the your child/children ask them question to make sure they understand how to read a compass.

*There are many other ways to teach this skill. Do your reach and figure out which way makes the most sense for your child/children.*

## Activity 3

There are a few different ways to do this activity. I will go over the ways you can do this activity.

Step 1:

Take your child/children on a nature walk in local woods or forest. Have them show you any tracks they may find during your walk. Then using a field guide(if needed) tell them what animal made the track and some basic facts about the animal.

After doing this for a few weeks have your child/children start telling you about the animal tracks you find during your walks. You can give your child/children a journal to make drawing of the tracks and write the information you gave them about each animal.

Step 2:

Using the internet or draw the prints of the animal .Make your child/children a matching game. This will help if you live in a place that you can not get out and walk year round. It will help you keep the information in their minds.

When playing the matching game you can also have them answer a question about the animal's track they matched before they can claim the match. This will help reinforce the information that you are teaching them.

Step 3:

Have your child/children draw the prints of the animals they have seen. Then have them tell you any other information about the animal that they can.

Step 4:

You can make a little test about the tracks animals make. Have them draw the prints or ask them questions about the information you have given them about the different animals.

You can also do this activity with eatable berries or plants. This will help if you child/children is ever lost in the woods and needs to find food.

## Activity 4

This is an activity that you can do along with some of the other activities in this book. It is one I think will help them if they ever need to hunt for food. Some children will not find it easy but it is one of the simplest activities in this book.

Have your child/children move off the trail and into the woods or open area you found. Have them try to move through the field with out making any noise. Which means no talking.(This is the part that some children have a problem doing.)

Make it a game to have them move from one side of the area to the other with out anyone around them hearing them. If you have a group of children have them all hide except one. Have this child walk around the area as quite as they can and found the other children. This will help all the children learn how important it can be to stay quite when needed.

This can help your child/children in many survival scenarios.

## Activity 5

This activity you most have a parent with them. This activity is one that is for children of at least 9 years of age if not older. Have the child/children learn to collect scrapes and wood for a small fire.

Teach them the different ways to make fire with or with out traditional methods.

Step 1:

Teach your child/children about collecting kindling and small sticks to get a fire started before you put on the bigger sticks/logs.

Step 2:

Teach your child/children how to lite a match or use a lighter the correct way.

Step 3:

Teach your child/children ways to make fire without a lighter or matches. Some examples are :

Battery and paper
Mirror and the sun

Make sure you have an adult with each child doing this activity. You can also use the internet or other survival book to find different ways you can make fire without matches or a lighter.

## Activity 6

This activity will cost you some money. But you can go to the dollar store or discount store to get many of the items your child/children will need. Have them take an old book bag and turn it into a Bug out bag. Then take your child/children to the store and help them pick out the items

they may need for their bag.
As you go around the store
with your child/children have
them tell you why they pick
the items they do for their bag.

Teach them about things
they may want to have in their
bug out bag such as a trap,
rope, water, cook set, eating
utensil, water bottle, bandana,
water proof matches, and some
basic food.

## Activity 7

This is also an activity that it would be best to have an adult with each child doing the activity. You can do one big basic teaching group demo and then break up into adult/child groupings to do the activity.

There are a few thing you will have to have for this

activity. They are rope and a trap. Any size will work but it would be best to have them work with the size they or you have in your bug out bag. I would said an 6' by 8'.

The first group demo would be showing the group of parents and children how to make a shelter with just rope and the trap. Then the second demo can have several parts because there are many types of shelters that can be made out of things found in the woods/forest.(Check out the internet for more information about different types of emergency shelters)

Step 1:

Have the child/adult group build a shelter with only the rope and trap.

Step 2:

Have the pairing build a shelter with the trap as the floor. (It will be easier to keep your body heat if you are not laying on the ground.)

Step 3:

Have the pair come up with their own idea of a shelter. That they can then spend the night sleeping in. After the night in their shelter have the pair talk about ways they can fix or improve their shelter.

## Activity 8

This activity has some different ways it can be taught. It is very important that children learn to get clean water to drink in a survival event. You can teach them a few different ways to clean and purify the water they find before they drink it.

Step 1:

Have the child/children use a life straw to drink the water they find. Give them instruction as to the correct way to use this survival tool.

Step 2:

Since your child/children should know how to make a fire teach them the correct way to boil water. Make sure they know that you can not put some things into or on a fire.

Step 3:

Teach the children how to make a filter out of things they

may have in their own bug out
bag.

There are many way to
teach your child/children how
to clean their water. You can
use the internet to research this
topic to found the way you
would like to teach your
child/children.

## Activity 9

This activity is one way that you can teach your child/children to catch their own food.

Step 1:

You will need to get some snare wire for this part of the

activity. Take your child/children into the woods or your backyard and set some small snare traps to catch small game. Show them how to set these snare and then after leaving them out over night check them the traps. If you have caught something then you can show your child/children how to clean and cook their own meal over an open fire.

Step 2:

For this activity you will need fishing line and a hook. Show your child/children how using a stick, fishing line, and the hook to make a fishing rod.

Take them to a small pond or stream and have them make their own rod to caught their own meal. Again after they have a fish teach them how to clean the fish and cook it themselves over a fire that they should be able to make themselves.

Step 3:

Have your child/children make a fire and cook what they find in their surrounding for their meal. (Parent supervision needed) Make sure you watch them to make sure they clean the food the right way.

Activity 10

This is the activity that puts what your child/children have learned all together into an overnight trip of survival.

Step 1:

Have your child/children pack their own Bug out bag

with what they think they will need for an overnight survival trip.

Step 2:

Then take them somewhere they can spend the night and just using what they pack have them spend the night in nature.

*Parents can pack their own over night survival bag. Watch over your child/children during the survival over night trip but try not to help them if it is not a life threatening event.*

Note page 1

Note page 2

If you would like more information on these activities or want to see more activities follow me at www.ednastowell.tumblr.com

You can also check out my other books on Amazon.com. Just search my name and enjoy the different SHTF e-books or paper backs.

# New Survival/ prepping book coming December 2015

Bug out bags for children

www.ingramcontent.com/pod-product-compliance
Lightning Source LLC
Chambersburg PA
CBHW061804280526
45787CB00003BA/1470